T0210103

A Mommy's Embrace

Bridgett Brennan

AuthorHouse™
1663 Liberty Drive
Bloomington, IN 47403
www.authorhouse.com
Phone: 1 (800) 839-8640

© 2018 Bridgett Brennan. All rights reserved.

No part of this book may be reproduced, stored in a retrieval system, or transmitted by any means without the written permission of the author.

Published by AuthorHouse 09/08/2018

ISBN: 978-1-5462-5928-2 (hc)
ISBN: 978-1-5462-5927-5 (sc)
ISBN: 978-1-5462-5926-8 (e)

Library of Congress Control Number: 2018910590

Print information available on the last page.

This book is printed on acid-free paper.

Because of the dynamic nature of the Internet, any web addresses or links contained in this book may have changed since publication and may no longer be valid. The views expressed in this work are solely those of the author and do not necessarily reflect the views of the publisher, and the publisher hereby disclaims any responsibility for them.

authorHOUSE®

Get to know the author!

Hello!

I am so excited to have this golden opportunity to share with you this dream from my heart, my very first book on paper into someone else's hands. I am a wife of one, mother of two, and grandmother of four. I have always loved to write and express myself through poetry- an avenue to release or reveal the words of life i have lived. Every year I would write my children "Christmas Letters" that shared with them about that years adventurers with each of them, the joys, disappointments, laughter and mostly how proud I was to be chosen to be their mommy and given the gift of watching them grow. I would hide the letter inside the tree and it was always the first thing they would open first! My son now is 29 and a father of 2, my daughter is now 25 and a mother of 2. My g-babies range from 8, 6, 4 and 1 ½. This is also the 20th year of marriage my husband and I now share. I am so blessed to be with the love of my life. I pray from my heart you are able to understand that this book represents my life. The colors represents all people that are portrayed throughout these pages- no one baby gender- no particular race of people- only focus on the one thing we all share "The Embrace"! The embrace of a life only a loving mother can give and hand down from her heart. Thank you for allowing me to live my dream because I have many obstacles with my health. At age 46 and the plate that was placed before me at birth I can honestly write to each of you metaphorically and say... *maybe the vegetables on your plate growing up tasted awful*but they fed you health, strength, energy, and wisdom. Well, my plate could not and cannot have just any "vegetables" on it! I had to learn in my 46 years that each "plate" contains a different style or type of meal, each and every meal for every individual. I have Chronic

Crohns Disease, Neuropathy (all over), a Vascular Neurosis (also all over), Osteoporosis, Osteoarthritis, Osteopenia, Cushing's Syndrome, 2 kidney disorders and active MRSA that prevents things like removing cataracts, and teeth. I was diagnosed in 1990 with Chronic Crohn's Disease and have been on prednisone every since with several other "vegetables" on my plate. Also I had a blood clot in my left leg that has caused me to be on coumadine as well. All I can say is by knowing I was able to share my dream with you thru these pages (and the ones to come) placed onto your plate of life I have truly been fed the greatness the Lord Jesus (I believe in) has nurtured me with- which is His nutrition from His great banquet that I believe we are all blessed to fill our plates with all the vegetables we need. Our families, friends, kind acts, caring people who care for people, as well as, Dr.'s, nurses, teachers, and *ALL faiths. Again I give thanks to Jesus whom I , my loving husband who supports and loves me endlessly. My children who helped me grow and expand my own life's journey. My g-babies, that I love so very much, who broadens my heart everyday with no end in sight to it. Whom I wish would slow down growing just a little. My Parents(where it truly all began I love and thank you for so much in my 46 years) and my Pastors (my family..I love you for the support and faith)

And on a P.S. moment to the illustrator, Jr. Greer for his artistic talent and *hard work* displayed in my first book. Thank you all!

From the author,

Bridgett Brennan

2brennan@bellsouth.net

1-405-693-1001

About The Illustrator

I have been in the arts ever since
I can remember. I have always loved
To draw, and paint and watch
The ideas in my mind come to life on paper.
My soul purpose is to see the
Creativity that Papa Yahweh
(God) has given everyone, being released
Into the world. To shine a light
In the darkness we face.
My advice for us all...
Get out there and create!
Love, J.R. Greer

Want to know more? Checkout my website
www.kraspedonarts.com

-The Embrace-
Not the race,
Not a skin color,
or
a living place
Focus only on
A mommy's embrace

Here's where we begin our journey Mommy and sweet angel you

We take these steps together
Mommy's embrace
between the love of
us two

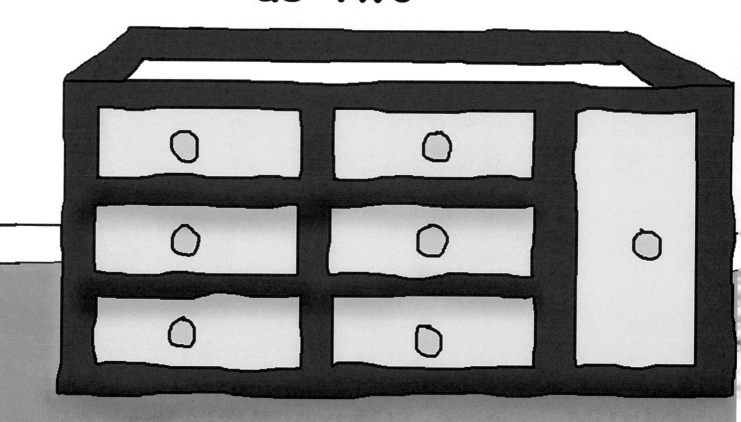

Welcome to your new home

Mommy's
Angel Charm

Oh how I've waited Anxiously to embrace your tiny warmth

To Feel your tiny heart beating while resting next to mine

I'm so excited holding you, embracing our quite time

This is your
Debut!
Mommy's
greatest
wish has
came true.

Such sweet peace
my special
prize
from oh so tiny
you

Mommy's heart overflows while tears of joy roll with unconditional love

Mommy's amazing
gift from the
best treasure chest
that belongs
to heaven above.

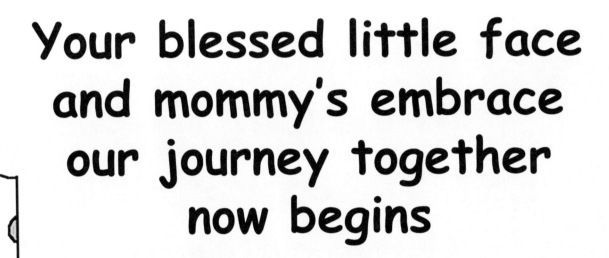

Your blessed little face
and mommy's embrace
our journey together
now begins

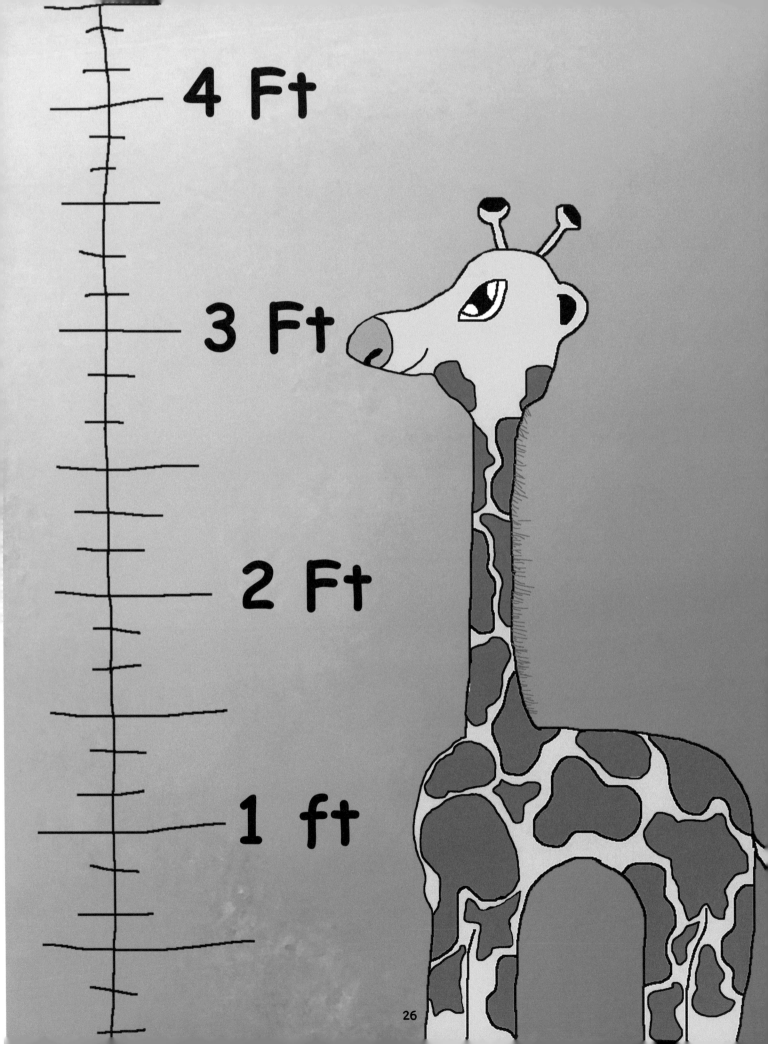

4 Ft

3 Ft

2 Ft

1 ft

So my sweet
little one
as you grow
all the while know

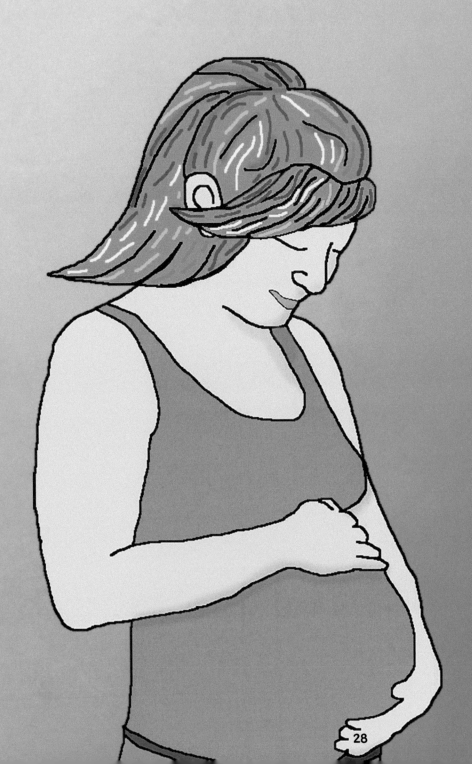

28

Your mommy's
embrace
will never
end

Keep your eyes open
Ask for book 2
The Journey you'll find
Maybe your journey too!

Printed in the United States
By Bookmasters